D0101915

THIS WALKER BOOK BELONGS TO:

Wester Hailes
Education Centre
School Library
5 Murrayburn Drive
Edinburgh EH14 2SU

40608

First published in *Smelly Jelly Smelly Fish* (1986), *Under the Bed* (1986),
Hard Boiled Legs (1987) and *Spollyollydiddlytiddlyitis* (1987)
by Walker Books Ltd, 87 Vauxhall Walk, London SE11 5HJ

This edition published 1997

4 6 8 10 9 7 5

Text © 1986, 1987 Michael Rosen
Illustrations © 1986, 1987 Quentin Blake
Cover illustration © 1997 Quentin Blake

This book has been typeset in Monotype Bembo.

Printed in Hong Kong/China

British Library Cataloguing in Publication Data
A catalogue record for this book is
available from the British Library.

ISBN 0-7445-5438-1

Tea in the Sugar Bowl, Potato in My Shoe

POEMS BY

Michael Rosen

ILLUSTRATED BY

Quentin Blake

WALKER BOOKS
AND SUBSIDIARIES
LONDON · BOSTON · SYDNEY

WESTER HAILES
EDUCATION CENTRE
SCHOOL LIBRARY
5 MURRAYBURN DRIVE
EDINBURGH EH14 2SU

CONTENTS

BREAKFAST TIME

Someone's dropped a bottle of milk,
the dustman's dropped a dustbin.
Someone's found a piece of potato in their shoe,
the baby's eating a sock.
When is it?
Breakfast time.

The cat's on the table eating someone's bacon,
someone's wiped butter on their trousers.
Someone's poured tea into the sugar bowl,
the baby is eating eggshells.
When is it?
Breakfast time.

Someone thinks they're going to get very angry,
someone thinks they're going crazy.
Someone thinks they're going to scream,
the baby has tipped cornflakes over its head.
When is it?
Breakfast time.

MESSING ABOUT

"Do you know what?"
said Jumping John.
"I had a bellyache
and now it's gone."

"Do you know what?"
said Kicking Kirsty.
"All this jumping
has made me thirsty."

"Do you know what?"
said Mad Mickey.
"I sat in some glue
and I feel all sticky."

"Do you know what?"
said Fat Fred.
"You can't see me,
I'm under the bed."

ON THE BEACH

There's a man over there
and he's sitting in the sand.
He buried himself at tea-time,
now he's looking for his hand.

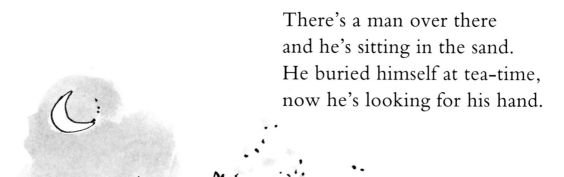

There's a boy over there
and he's sitting on the rocks,
eating apple crumble,
washing dirty socks.

There's a woman over there
sitting in the sea.
I can see her
but she can't see me.

There's a girl over there
and she's sitting on a chair.
Standing just behind her
is a big grizzly bear.

13

WHAT IF...

What if
they made children-sized diggers
and you could take them down to the beach
to dig really big holes
and great big sandcastles
that the waves couldn't knock down.

What if
they made children-sized submarines
you could get into and go off underwater
looking at people's feet
and you could find old wrecked ships
and glide about
finding treasure.

What if
they made children-sized helicopters
that you took with you to the beach
so that you could take off in one of them
whenever you wanted to
and fly about above the beach
or up the cliffs
looking into those high-up caves
and swoop down again
towards the sea and some secret beach.

What if
they made children-sized ice-creams...

FEELING ILL

Lying in the middle of the bed
waiting for the clock to change
flicking my toes on the sheets
watching a plane cross the window
staring at the glare of the light
smelling the orange on the table
counting the flowers on the curtain
holding my head with my hand
hearing the steps on the stairs
lying in the middle of the bed
waiting for the clock to change.

DOWN AT THE DOCTOR'S

Down at the doctor's
where everybody goes
there's a fat white cat
with a dribbly bibbly nose,
with a dribble dribble here
and a bibble bibble there,
that's the way
she dribbles her nose.

Down at the doctor's
where everybody goes
there's a fat black dog
with messy missy toes,
with a mess mess here
and a miss miss there,
that's the way
she messes her toes.

Down at the doctor's
where everybody goes
there's a fat red parrot
who everybody knows,
with a hi-de-hi here
and a how-de-how there,
that's the parrot
that everybody knows.

IF BEDS HAD WINGS

What if
my bed grew wings and I could fly away in my bed.
I would fly to the top of a high block of flats,
look out over all the streets
and then come floating slowly down to the ground.

I would fly to a misty island near Japan
and watch fishing boats cross the sea.

If my bed grew wings I would fly to a thick forest
where there was an old broken–down castle
that no one knew about, hidden in the trees.
And wherever I went
and whatever I saw,
all the time I was in my bed.

OVER MY TOES

Over my toes
goes
the soft sea wash
see the sea wash
the soft sand slip
see the sea slip
the soft sand slide
see the sea slide
the soft sand slap
see the sea slap
the soft sand wash
over my toes.

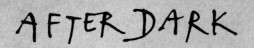

AFTER DARK

Outside after dark
trains hum and traffic lights wink
after dark, after dark.

In here after dark
curtains shake and cupboards creak
after dark, after dark.

Under the covers after dark
I twiddle my toes and hug my pillow
after dark, after dark.

MORE WALKER PAPERBACKS
For You to Enjoy

WE'RE GOING ON A BEAR HUNT
by Michael Rosen/Helen Oxenbury

Winner of the Smarties Book Prize and Highly Commended for
the Kate Greenaway Medal

"A dramatic and comic masterpiece… Beautifully produced, written and
illustrated, this is a classic." *The Independent on Sunday*

0-7445-2323-0   £4.99

LITTLE RABBIT FOO FOO
by Michael Rosen/Arthur Robins

A new version of a popular playground rhyme.

"Simple and hilarious… I laugh every time I think about it."
Susan Hill, The Sunday Times

0-7445-2065-7   £4.99

WHO'S BEEN SLEEPING IN MY PORRIDGE?
by Colin McNaughton

A book of daft poems and pictures.

"A sort of high quality Beano gone absolutely potty, which any child
over five will adore." *The Sunday Telegraph*

0-7445-2361-3   £6.99

Walker Paperbacks are available from most booksellers, or by post from B.B.C.S., P.O. Box 941, Hull, North Humberside HU1 3YQ
24 hour telephone credit card line 01482 224626

To order, send: Title, author, ISBN number and price for each book ordered, your full name and address,
cheque or postal order payable to BBCS for the total amount and allow the following for postage and packing:
UK and BFPO: £1.00 for the first book, and 50p for each additional book to a maximum of £3.50.
Overseas and Eire: £2.00 for the first book, £1.00 for the second and 50p for each additional book.

Prices and availability are subject to change without notice.